WITHDRAWAL

BiZARRE VeHICLES

Michael J. Rosen

and Ben Kassoy

Illustrations by Pat Sandy

M Millbrook Press • Minneapolis

Millbrook Press
A division of Lerner Publishing Group, Inc.
241 First Avenue North
Minneapolis, MN 55401 U.S.A.

Website address: www.lernerbooks.com

Main body text set in Adrianna Regular 12/16
Typeface provided by Chank

Library of Congress Cataloging-in-Publication Data

Rosen, Michael J., 1954–
    Bizarre vehicles / by Michael J. Rosen and Ben Kassoy ; illustrated by Pat Sandy.
      p.   cm. — (No way!)
    Includes index.
    ISBN 978–0–7613–8985–9 (lib. bdg. : alk. paper)
    ISBN 978–1–4677–1704–5 (eBook)
    1. Vehicles—Miscellanea—Juvenile literature. 2. Transportation—Miscellanea—Juvenile literature. I. Kassoy, Ben. II. Sandy, Pat, ill. III. Title.
TL147.R649 2014
629.04'6—dc23   2012045903

Manufactured in the United States of America
1 – BP – 7/15/13

The authors would like to recognize the generous contribution of Christoffer Strömstedt, as well as the efforts of Ashley Heestand, Colin Stoecker, and Claire Hamilton in the researching, fact-checking, and drafting of the No Way! series of books.

TABLE of CONTENTS

BiKE TO THE FUTURE
MONOVELO

You're cruising around in something that resembles a giant glowing doughnut. Sounds like science fiction, right?

Not so fast! This futuristic form of transportation has already rolled out! Introducing the monovelo! It may look out-of-this-world, but like many things, it was made in China.

Picture a 6.5-foot-tall (1.9-meter) doughnut. That's the monovelo's frame. You sit in the doughnut hole, where you'll find the only normal parts of this wacky wheel: handles for holding and pedals for pedaling.

Helmet on? Off you go! Unfortunately, your top speed is 12 miles (19 kilometers) per hour. So you may have trouble keeping up with friends on bikes.

Riding a monovelo is pretty easy. As on a bike, you pedal the monovelo. As on a motorcycle, you lean to turn your vehicle left or right. And as on an alien spaceship, you get to glow in the dark.

Equipped with a series of interwoven lights, a moving monovelo resembles a glowing wheel. Colors course around and around as it spins. At the 2008 Olympics in Beijing, China, more than one hundred monovelos lit up the closing ceremonies.

Want one? That'll be about $2,000, plus a few hundred for shipping and handling. Or for just $1,790, you can buy a monovelo without the lights. But then, that's like a doughnut with no icing.

A monovelo rolls at the 2008 Olympic Games in Beijing, China.

WALKING—ER, BOUNCING—ON WATER
AQUASKIPPER

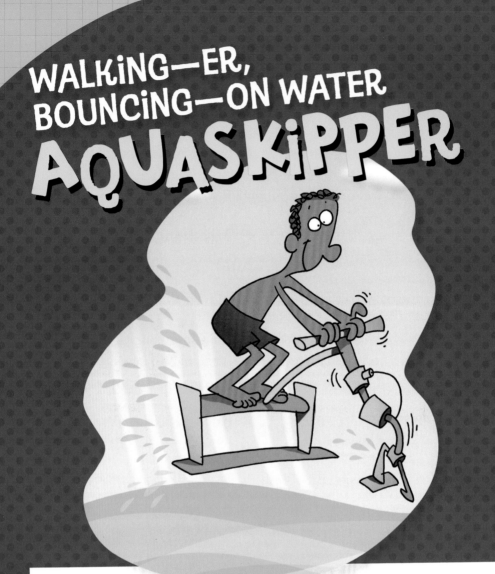

Waterskiing or wakeboarding are exciting means of water travel—
if you have a friend with a boat. Without a motor, you're sunk.

But there's another option. You can "fly" solo across the sea on
the AquaSkipper: a human-powered hydrofoil!

Wait up. Here's a quick and totally un-boring scientific
explanation of the hydrofoil. It's like an airplane wing for a water
vehicle. As the vehicle's speed increases, water pushes up on
the wing. With enough speed, the wing actually lifts the vehicle
up and out of the water. That means water isn't dragging on
the vehicle, so it can speed up faster. And that means more,
woo-hoo! I'm flying!

See how un-boring science is?

The 25-pound (11-kilogram) AquaSkipper is about 6 feet (1.8 m) long. How does it work? First, imagine a bike plus a water ski plus a pogo stick. You stand on a platform and hold the handlebars. Then pretend you're coasting on a bicycle. But instead of bike wheels, your AquaSkipper is equipped with hydrofoils. The front one aids in steering. The rear one helps it float. To build speed, you hop up and down. This isn't just walking on water—you're jumping on it!

You're skimming across the water at speeds reaching 17 miles (27 km) per hour. (The fastest swimmers reach about 5 miles [8 km] per hour—for very short bursts.) So now you can tell your friends, "Eat my bubbles!"

A man stays afloat on an AquaSkipper.

PUT SOME SPRING IN YOUR STEP
POWERBOCKS

You can dunk a basketball! You can run a lap in under a minute! You can perform five backflips in a row!

Maybe in your dreams.

Or . . . maybe *in your driveway!* All you need is a pair of PowerBocks, a shoe that combines stilts and a pogo stick.

Your feet are secured in bindings. Picture what holds your boots on a snowboard. Your feet are connected to a rubber footpad by a fiberglass spring. Picture the bottom tip of a pogo stick. PowerBocks make you half human, half superhuman. Say: *Boing! Boing!*

Now you've got some serious spring in your step! You can soar up to 6 feet (1.8 m) in the air. You can run 20 miles (32 km) per hour. Your strides are 9 feet (2.7 m) long.

With a lot of practice, PowerBocks help people pull off some amazing moves.

The most skilled "Bockers" can execute amazing, acrobatic moves. They somersault down sidewalks. They leap over cars. They tell gravity, "Hey, you're not the boss of me!"

PowerBocks are named after Alexander Bock, who invented the fantastic footwear in the 1990s. Since then, they've had many nicknames and inspired many imitations. They're known as jumping stilts, powerskips, powerisers, and power stilts. In Australia, they're kangaroo boots. But wherever you're from, they're out of this world!

As a sport, PowerBocking takes walking to new extremes. As a form of physical fitness, it makes jogging feel like sleepwalking. And as a means of rescuing kittens from trees, it affords firefighters a little more naptime.

Now it's your turn. Sure, you can walk the walk. But can you Bock the Bock?

ROCKETMAN
PERSONAL JETPACK

Every so often, science fiction becomes nonfiction. Are there flying cars? Mmm...not yet. Are there jetpacks to fly you through the air? Mmm...you bet! They're real. And they're just as cool as you imagined them.

Resembling a mini-rocket, the Martin Jetpack brands itself as the world's first practical jetpack. At a cost of $100,000, you practically need to be a millionaire to afford it.

Strap yourself into this 254-pound (115 kg) combination helicopter-backpack and fly up, up, and away. You can soar for thirty minutes and 30 miles (48 km) at a height of 8,000 feet (2,438 m). That's about a quarter as high as most airliners fly. (Unfortunately, the Martin Jetpack doesn't offer an in-flight beverage service.)

Don't have your sights set on height? Have a need for speed, instead? Try Jet Pack International's H202-Z. This lightweight speed demon can only climb to 250 feet (76 m). Its flights last for just thirty-three seconds. But the H202-Z can zoom at 75 miles (121 km) per hour. That would be considered speeding on most freeways—but you'd be flying *over* them.

Or try a Jetlev, a water jetpack. It's a little like waterskiing. You're tied to a long tube that's pulled behind a boat. Water is sucked up and surges out of the jetpack with such force that it can lift you 30 feet (9.1 m) high. On a Jetlev, you can soar like a bird and skim the water like a skipped stone. You'll rock!

Jetlevs give you a wet and wild good time.

A WHALE OF A GOOD TIME
SOLO SUBMARINE

Do you go overboard—*splash!*—for the ocean? Can't wait to wade into marine biology? Eager to explore the underwater wonders of the world? Thanks to this pair of wet and wild watercrafts, you're all set to get in over your head!

Next time you're on an airliner climbing into the clouds, check out the magazine in the seat pocket. The Hammacher Schlemmer catalog offers the Personal Sub, a vehicle that will take you on a trip in the other direction.

The sub may sound like a foot-long (0.3 m) sandwich layered with meats and cheeses. Nope! It's a 4.7-foot (1.4 m) sphere that takes you and a friend on a six-hour tour of coral reefs and shipwrecks.

You control the sub with a joystick. Think of playing a video game. Yet no game can provide this kind of aquatic adventure—even if your flat-screen TV were waterproof.

If you want a shark's speed, check out the Seabreacher. This sub only sinks 5 feet (1.5 m) below the surface, but it travels 25 miles (40 km) per hour. Rise to the surface, and this lean, mean submarine cruises at 50 miles (80 km) per hour!

And when we said "shark," we weren't kidding: Seabreacher owners can customize the paint jobs on their subs to resemble sharks. Or dolphins. Or killer whales. The Seabreacher not only looks like a sea creature—it can leap several feet out of the water!

You may be afraid of sharks, but in a Seabreacher, you'll be one of them!

Ahoy! This Seabreacher looks like a dolphin.

SWIMSUIT OPTIONAL
SKYSURFING

Snowboarding probably isn't the most practical way to travel. Neither is skydiving. Put the two together, and you get one of the *most* impractical ways of getting around. But you also get one of the most fun!

It's called skysurfing, the best of both sports. As with skydiving, you decide—for whatever reason—to leap out of a perfectly good airplane in midair. As with surfing, you ride the waves on a board. Except, now they're air waves instead of ocean waves!

Your board is like a snowboard. But you'll never be bored on this wild trip. You don't just free-fall before opening your parachute, you free-twirl, free-flip, free-barrel roll— you're as free as the wind.

Skysurfing is a rare chance to move in four dimensions. Soar up and down. Zip backward and forward. Slide side to side. Zoom slower or faster. Skysurfing is also a rare opportunity to shout, "Gnarly, dude!" at an altitude of 10,000 feet (3,050 m).

Think you can manage more mixing and matching midair? You're ready for BASE jumping. Strap on a parachute. Maybe even skis and a wingsuit. BASE is an acronym for building, antenna, span (bridges), and earth (cliffs). Those are the four surfaces from which these adventurers jump with a parachute.

Some BASE jumpers wear skis and a wingsuit. After some aerial acrobatics, you kick off your skis—*"Ski you later!"* With your wingsuit, you're like a bat!

Or maybe you're just batty.

A wingsuit slows a jumper's fall, so the fun trip lasts a bit longer.

KERALA SNAKE BOAT

What glides through the water, stretches over 100 feet (30 m) long, and sings?

Yikes! You'll be glad to know the answer is not a sort of serpent or water predator. Still, Kerala snake boats are monstrous. They're among the longest wooden boats in the world.

Snake boat races need a lot of paddlers.

Snake boats are built in Kerala, a state in southwest India. They resemble aquatic reptiles. They range in length from 100 to 143 feet (30 to 44 m). The back, or stern, can be 20 feet (6 m) high, which gives it the look of a snake rising from the water. You'd expect to hear, "Quick, everyone, get to shore!" And you'd expect some serious hissing.

Instead, you'll hear singing! Displayed at festivals, the boats can carry crews that exceed one hundred: sixty paddlers paddle, ten helmsmen steer, and two dozen singers chant. Their music rocks the boat—and keeps everyone in paddling rhythm.

Before their days as a floating musical, these boats played a military role. The Kerala region is home to forty-four rivers. The rivers were the battleground—battle*water*—among nearby towns. One day, a leader must have thought, "Hey, what if my whole army could float on one boat?"

Today, neighboring villages still battle it out on snake boats. Only now, they don't fight to the death—they fight to the finish line.

On your mark, get set, paddle!

GO OVERBOARD!
RINSPEED SQUBA

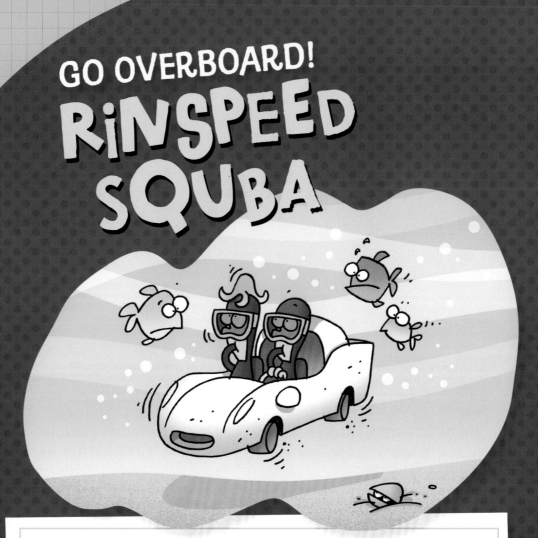

In 1977, James Bond, Agent 007, escaped from the bad guys in his super-cool, super-stealthy combination car-submarine. But that was in the movie *The Spy Who Loved Me*. Recently, the movie has come to life. A similar amphibious vehicle is real!

Sleek and white, the Rinspeed sQuba cruises up to 75 miles (121 km) per hour on land. It looks like a luxury convertible. A driver can even steer the sQuba from afar using a remote control. It's like playing a video game! Except it's not a video. And it's not a game.

Plus, you can take it off-roading. At the push of a button, the sQuba switches from *vroom-vroom* to *splish-splash*. It doubles as a submarine! Instead of cruising downtown, you're cruising down, down, down—three stories below the surface.

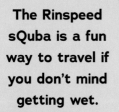

The Rinspeed sQuba is a fun way to travel if you don't mind getting wet.

Hey, wait! The top is still down! Chill out. As the car fills with water, it moves beneath the surface. You're driving—and diving! The car comes with built-in masks and air tanks so you can breathe. A bathing suit is not standard equipment, so do plan ahead.

Want to get wet but need something bigger? Then go with the Terra Wind. It's a combination yacht and motor coach. Just picture a 42-foot (13 m), 15-ton (14-metric-ton) mobile home that can swim. Or picture a million-dollar boat with a giant hot tub, a big-screen TV, and a full kitchen—that you can drive to the supermarket to restock the fridge. The Terra Wind proves that bigger is better—and wetter!

The Terra Wind doesn't look like a boat, but it floats like one.

ON A ROLL
ZORBING

Tumbling down a hill can be fun. *If* you don't mind grass stains. Or in the case of Jack and Jill, a broken crown.

So join a rolling revolution called Zorbing! All you do is climb inside a transparent plastic sphere that's 10 feet (3 m) in diameter and—have a ball! You're like a giant happy hamster!

Actually, a Zorb is a ball inside a ball. A pocket of air separates the two, which softens the impact of your bumpy ride. But nothing keeps you from having a wild trip. With a hearty push from the outside and a little help from gravity, you're going around and down and over and onward!

A harness keeps you safely inside the ball. On a steep hill, a Zorb can travel 30 miles (48 km) per hour. And there are no brakes on this thing! Unless you count petering out on flatland.

Zorbing courses are good places to get your roll on!

Want to ride on more than air? In hydro-Zorbing, about 5 gallons (19 liters) of water are pumped inside the ball. Now you can slip, slide, and slosh down the course. No harness needed!

These little globes are loved all over our big globe. From the United States to Australia, Zorbing parks offer topsy-turvy courses. Zig and zag! Twist and turn!

Zorbing is a way to get around. It's also an afternoon of thrills. And it's a sport with prizes for winners. Can you stand the challenge? Remain upright throughout the entire ride and you win! Hate to burst your bubble, though: staying up is tough!

SHANGHAi MAGLEV TRAiN

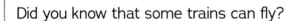

Did you know that some trains can fly?

One in particular soars above the rest. That's the Shanghai Maglev Train in China. It flies in two ways. First, it goes really, really fast. We're talking the fastest train in the world. It reaches 310 miles (499 km) per hour! That's more than a third of the speed of sound. And second, the Maglev *literally* files. No, seriously. It travels a few inches above the track.

Maglev is an abbreviation of "magnetic levitation." This technology uses magnets to lift and suspend the train just above the rails. Floating, there's no contact between train and track. That means friction doesn't slow the train. So that's flying *plus* flying!

In the time it takes to jump into a car, shut the doors, fasten the seat belts, start the car, and choose a radio station, the Maglev is already traveling 150 miles (241 km) per hour. When it's time to stop, the conductor must hit the brakes about 7 miles (11 km) from the station.

The world's fastest train is also the quietest, with just the refreshing *whoosh* of the air above the rails. And the ride's so smooth that passengers don't have to wear seat belts.

More trains to blow your brain? Switzerland's Glacier Express train is a 6,000-foot-high (1.8 km) trek through the picturesque Alps. The Pride of Africa train travels from South Africa to Egypt (luxury bedrooms, onboard shopping, and safari tours included!). After you hear "All aboard!" you may never want to get off.

The Shanghai Maglev Train carries people around China at superfast speeds.

WONDER WHEELS
ART CARS

When Harrod Blank got his first car at the age of sixteen, it was white—bland and boring.

Harrod was anything but boring. He painted a rooster on the door. He attached objects to the car's surface. He continued to paint, bolt, and glue until, years later, his Beetle vibrated with color. It bulged with globes, windmills, skulls, and a huge flag. It was only the first of his *art cars*, a term for vehicles that have been *steered* into works of art.

"Cartists" all over the world transform everyday rides into wonders on wheels. One well-known cartist is Brian Visker. His most famous work, *Oojah*, peers at spectators with many sets of foam eyes and noses. Its mouth reveals dozens of scary teeth. Talk about a monster truck!

Brian Visker's car *Oojah* turns heads when he drives it down the road.

Visker's works are among more than 250 featured each year at the Art Car Parade in Houston, Texas. Attendees stare in amazement and amusement as a full peacock car (feathers, beak, and all!) drives past. A guitar on wheels. A car encrusted with seashells. There are even decked-out lawn mowers. In this parade, they're a cut above the rest!

Houston is also home to the Art Car Museum. There, you'll find the world's largest collection of wild wheels, including the famous StuDENT Driver. One artist took a Buick that his grandmother had wrecked and turned the clunker into a classic. The entire car is buried beneath road signs, a parking meter, a telephone pole, a mangled bicycle, and even a stuffed raccoon.

Looks like some cars should be in a gallery—and off the road!

Harrod Blank drives his Beetle.

WINGS ARE FOR THE BIRDS
FLYING SAUCER

It's disk-shaped. A dome covers its cockpit. It hovers off the ground and zooms through the air. It must be a UFO!

Or just an FO, because this flying object *is* identified. The Moller Neuera is your personal flying saucer! This space-age vehicle proves the future is now.

Like a helicopter, the aircraft takes off and lands vertically. Unlike a helicopter, the Neuera doesn't need giant propellers. It's only 10 feet (3 m) in diameter and 3 feet (0.9 m) high, but this mighty machine can lift itself off the ground.

So you're up, up, and flying—and flying fast! The Neuera can soar at 100 miles (161 km) per hour. Say, bye-bye, birdies!

The Neuera's onboard computers ensure that it doesn't enter government airspace. So, unlike most aircrafts, you don't need permission to fly it. Or even a pilot's license. You're above the law! Or—because it only goes about 10 feet (3 m) high—you're sort of below it.

This is an early version of the Moller personal flying saucer.

In the future, this two-seat saucer could be used for military, law enforcement, or emergency rescue purposes. But until then, it simply provides the coolest way to get around the block or to go with your Halloween alien costume.

Moller International's latest invention is a mini-plane that can soar 300 miles (483 km) per hour. The Moller Skycar could replace regular cars someday. "No traffic, no red lights, no speeding tickets," says the inventor.

Some say the sky's the limit. This company says there's no limit!

Someday soon we may see people going to work and school in Moller's Skycar.

TRIP TO NOWHERE
FLIGHTLESS AIRBUS

The humongous Airbus A300 looks and feels like a regular airplane. Comfy seats. Fold-down tray tables. Flight crew.

But the plane hasn't taken off in several years. Still, hundreds of passengers board each weekend.

Bahadur Chand Gupta grew up in a poor Indian village where few had seen a plane (except in movies). But Gupta was obsessed with planes, and he eventually became a mechanical engineer for Indian Airlines. Fellow villagers frequently asked him about flying. (Once, Gupta tried to sneak a friend onto a flight—he was caught.)

Twenty-eight years later, Gupta had a safer, if not saner, idea. Can't bring villagers to the plane? Bring the plane to the villagers. So he purchased a broken-down plane, took it apart, and shipped it cross-country. Then he spent two years rebuilding it. Welcome aboard!

Thousands of schoolchildren and adults from far and wide travel to the plane that doesn't travel. Most will never take an actual flight. This simulation is the closest they'll come to flying the friendly skies.

Likewise, this plane will never fly. (Try not to notice the missing wing and tail section.) Yet, the experience offered is thrilling. Gupta serves as pilot. His wife, Nirmal, is head flight attendant. They hand out boarding passes, demonstrate safety features, buckle each person's seat belt, and serve "in-flight" meals.

Even better, you don't have to wait in security lines. No air turbulence. Sure, inflate the life jackets. And exit the plane by bouncing down the emergency slide. Hope you enjoyed your flight!

Passengers on real flights usually don't get to exit the airplane by going down the emergency slide.

GLOSSARY

acronym: an abbreviation formed by the first letter of two or more words such as USA (United States of America) or LOL (laugh out loud)

adornment: ornaments added to an object or surface to enhance its beauty

aerial: living, growing, or occurring in the air

amphibious: capable of operating or living in water as well as on land

bizarre: remarkably strange

buoyancy: the ability of a body or object to float in a liquid

free-fall: dropping through the air with nothing lessening gravity's pull. Skydivers are in free fall before their parachutes are released.

friction: the rubbing of one thing against another

futuristic: being or resembling how something might look in the future

helmsman: a person who steers or helps control certain types of boats

picturesque: a scene so visually pleasing that it seems like the perfect subject for a beautiful painting

simulation: the enacting or imitating of a real-world experience in a practice situation that is as close to real as can be created

transparent: allowing light to pass through so objects behind can be seen

turbulence: choppy or unsteady movement of air or water; a disturbance

wingsuit: a type of jumping gear that increases a body's ability to stay aloft. Typically, the suit accomplishes this with fabric stretched between the arms and the body.

FURTHER READING

BOOKS

Fridell, Ron. *Seven Wonders of Transportation.* Minneapolis: Twenty-First Century Books, 2010.
This book traces remarkable forms of travel, from the London Underground to the grandest ocean liner, from ancient animal caravans to modern "supergreen cars."

Harris, Joseph. *Transportation: The Impact of Science and Technology.* New York: Gareth Stevens Publishing, 2010.
This book highlights the history of transportation technology, how transportation has changed the environment, and examines how we may get around in the future.

Waxman, Laura Hamilton. *Terrific Transportation Inventions.* Minneapolis: Lerner Publications Company, 2014.
Learn the fascinating stories behind the transportation inventions you use every day such as bicycles and cars.

WEBSITES

The Future Passed: Jetpack Edition
http://www.theverge.com/2011/11/3/2504531/jetpack-history-future-passed
Check out this smart, witty, and fact-filled journey through the one-hundred-year history of the rocket belt. The site features graphics, photos, ads, and videos of the many attempts at propelling a human through the air.

Trotting the Globe
http://library.thinkquest.org/04oct/00450/weirdwonderful.htm
Trotting the Globe presents a brief history of air, water, and land travel. American and Australian fourth graders and fifth graders created this site, which includes a section on "the weird and wonderful," as well as interactive games and puzzles.

INDEX